First edition 2024



Author, Rising Heroes

Front & back cover by Rijah Sarmad, Hameeda Kassim

Published by Emaan Power, Australia

Website: www.emaanpower.com

# Book Creators

Khadija Faiq (Age 15 from Canada), Hameeda Kassim (Age 13 from Ireland), Ahmed Ahmed (Age 15 from UK), Yusuf Ahmed (Age 12 from UK), Muhammad Waabil (Age 15 from Pakistan), Sumayyah Hooria (Age 10 from UK), Abdullah Rashid (Age 12 from Australia), Maha Tola (Age 11 from Turkey), Lucas Gallardo (Age 9 from Australia), Nurkamila Safia (Age 11 from Malaysia), Mohammad Abdullah Umar (Age 13 from UAE), Zaynab Shakoor (Age 11 from Australia), Wajeeh Uddin (Age 12 from Pakistan), Ibrahim Hafiz (Age 12 from UK), Inara Sidra (Age 11 from UK), Musab Ahmed (Age 15 from UAE), Zaid Ahmed (Age 13 from UAE), Ayan Adnan (Age 14 from Qatar), Anwar (Age 9 from Netherland), Zainab Ahmad (Age 13 from UK), Noor Fatima (Age 10 from Pakistan), Zaahiya Rujub (Age 9 from Australia), Nana-Asmaou Shareef (Age 10 from France), Ayman Lawal (Age 11 from Australia), Hassan Cheema (Age 13 from UK), Rania Ibrahim (Age 10 from UAE), Ayaan Cheema (Age 9 from UK), Mustafa (Age 9 from Qatar), Hiba Omar (Age 9 from USA), Mohamad (Age 15 from USA), Khizer Azeem (Age 10 from Canada), Anisah Asha (Age 14 from UK), Zubair Ahmad (Age 11 from Ireland), Talha Ahmad (Age

9 from Ireland), Hassan Mustafa Khalifa (Age 11 from UK), Abyane Fall (Age 10 from USA), Aaliyan Umair (Age 8 from USA), Aaminah Hameed (Age 11 from USA), Sabriyah Idris (Age 13 from UAE), Muhammad Idris (Age 9 from UAE), Muhammad Novsarka (Age 12 from UK), Zainah (Age 10 from USA), Fatima Arif (Age 13 from Canada), Zara Shaheen (Age 11 from USA), Mysha Shaheen (Age 11 from USA), Rayan Mazin (Age 12 from USA), Fatima Abbasi (Age 12 from Canada), Hassan (Age 12 from USA), Ismahan (Age 10 from USA), Zoha Akhtar (Age 12 from USA), Safa Akhtar (Age 12 from USA), Usman (Age 14 from Canada), AbdurRahman (Age 13 from USA), Laily (Age 9 from UK), Shahpara (Age 12 from Canada),Hamzah Ansari (Age 10 from USA), Maryam Tariq (Age 14 from UAE), Abeera Abbasi (Age 14 from Canada), Faryal Ismail (Age 14 from UAE), Safia (Age 13 from Germany), Rijah Sarmad (Age 12 from Sweden), Dilem (Age 9 from UK), Ghazi (Age 9 from UAE), Bareen (Age 10 from Canada), Abdul Mateen (Age 12 from Brunei), Iman Barrie (Age 17 from USA), Adam Muhammad Schroeder (Age 11 from USA), Hanna (Age 10 from Brunei)

# Contents

# Foreword

*by Ariba Farheen, Founder of Emaan Power*

At Emaan Power, I'm driven by a singular vision: to unlock the unstoppable potential within young Muslims, turning them into unshakeable believers and powerful leaders who can transform the world. I didn't just want to create a program that teaches kids about their faith—I wanted to ignite a fire within them to live boldly, confidently, and with purpose. That's why I founded Emaan Power, where we deliver this vision through cutting-edge programs, online workshops, and real-world projects designed to inspire passion and drive.

But our mission doesn't stop with the kids. I'm committed to empowering moms too, providing them with the tools and insights to raise leaders who stand firm in their faith and make a real difference. We've already seen hundreds of kids step up, lead, and create lasting change in their communities. Emaan Power is where the next generation of Muslim leaders is forged, and the impact we're making is nothing short of extraordinary.

One of the most exciting projects we've completed is "Voices from Olives," a remarkable collection of stories written by young students from around the world, all part of our Rising Heroes program. In just 8 weeks, these students took complete ownership of this project—from the inception of the idea to the marketing of the book. Through this journey, they not only crafted narratives of resilience, hope, and courage but also discovered their own value and potential. Watching them grow into true leaders of change has been nothing short of inspiring.

This project is a powerful demonstration of what our children can achieve when we give them the right support, nurture their strengths, and provide them with opportunities to rise.

It shows the world that with the proper guidance and encouragement, young Muslims have the ability to make a significant impact, not just in their own communities but globally. Despite the fitna and challenges of our times, this project proves that we can still empower our children to overcome obstacles, stay true to their faith, and emerge as leaders who can create positive change. By empowering them to take ownership of their ideas and bring them to life, we're not only helping them realize their potential but also fostering the next generation of leaders ready to face the world's challenges head-on.

For more information about Emaan Power, please visit www.emaanpower.com.

# Introduction

In the midst of Palestine's ongoing conflict and suffering, there are stories that shine brightly with courage, resilience, and hope. This collection of personal narratives offers a deeply moving look into the lives of individuals who face immense challenges but still manage to inspire with their strength and determination.

In these pages, you will encounter tales of remarkable people who rise above their circumstances. From children who transform their passions into symbols of joy to those who bravely confront personal tragedies, each story is a testament to the enduring human spirit. These individuals not only navigate their hardships with remarkable fortitude but also find ways to bring light and positivity into their communities.

These narratives highlight the themes of perseverance and hope that define the Palestinian experience. Despite the overwhelming odds and daily struggles, these stories demonstrate how the human spirit can remain resilient and vibrant. They show that even in the face of conflict and adversity, people can find ways to spread kindness, chase their dreams, and hold on to hope.

As you read through these accounts, you'll see how these individuals turn their trials into sources of strength and inspiration. Their journeys remind us that, no matter how difficult life becomes, the essence of humanity—our ability to remain hopeful, loving, and compassionate—can shine through. Their stories are a powerful reminder that resilience can thrive even in the darkest of times.

# Who are Rising Heroes

This book is written by the Rising Heroes. Rising Heroes are a diverse group of children, aged 8 to 16, from all corners of the globe, united by their shared commitment to making a positive impact.

As students of Emaan Power, they have come together with a common goal: to use their talents and passion to amplify the voices of those who are often unheard. Through hard work and dedication, they have created this book about Palestine, entirely on their own, to shed light on the resilience and strength of the Palestinian people.

We encourage you to dive into these pages, absorb the stories that these young heroes have brought to life, and share this book with others. By reading and spreading their work, you too can be a part of this powerful movement for awareness and change.

May Allah bless and guide our Rising Heroes, granting them continued strength, wisdom, and compassion as they strive to make the world a better place. May their efforts be rewarded in this life and the hereafter. And may Allah protect and uplift the people of Palestine, granting them peace, justice, and the strength to endure with patience and faith. Ameen.

# The Story of Haytham Al Ashqar

By Shahpara
Comic by Abyane Fall

In the heart of Gaza, in a place called Al Nusairat, lived a young boy named Haytham. Like most kids his age, Haytham loved to play football with his friends, Obaida and Kareem. On a bright and sunny day, the three boys were kicking the ball around at the Al Jadeed refugee camp, laughing and having fun. But then, something terrible happened. Out of nowhere, a bomb hit the house next to them.

The explosion threw Haytham to the ground. In the chaos, he lost the lower part of his arm. He saw his hand on the ground, but there was nothing he could do. All he could think of was his mother. "Mama, mama!" he cried out as loud as he could. His mother rushed out, and when she saw what happened, she quickly took him to Al Awda Hospital. The doctors there wrapped his arm in a bandage.

But the pain of losing his arm was not the only pain Haytham felt that day. He learned that ten people had died in the bombing. Among them were his two best friends, Obaida and Kareem. Their young lives were taken away by the war, leaving Haytham to face the world without them.

As he recovered, Haytham's smile never faded. When people asked him what he wanted most, he didn't talk about his pain. Instead, he said, "I wish I could travel abroad to get a new hand, so I can help my mom and dad, and so I can play, write, and read again." When they asked where his lost hand was, Haytham simply said, "It's in Jannah." His trust in Allah made him believe that his hand was in a better place, and this belief brought him peace. Haytham didn't let his loss shake his faith; it made him stronger.

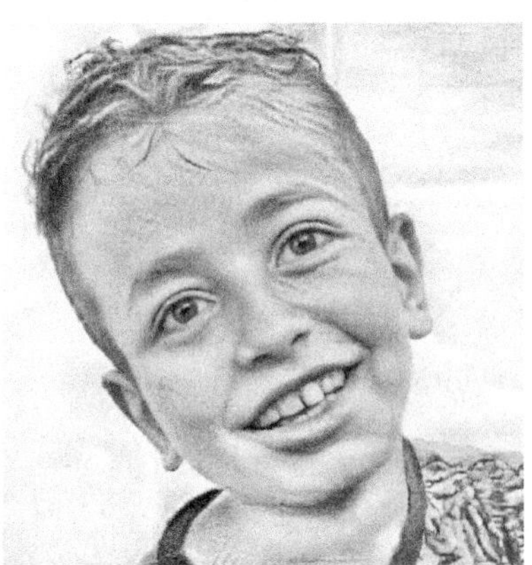

Now, imagine—if you lost a hand and your two best friends all in one day, how would you react? Most of us would feel angry, lost, and might even complain about the unfairness of it all. We often whine about much smaller problems. But Haytham was different. Despite all that had happened, he didn't get angry, he didn't complain. Instead, Haytham smiled. His faith in Allah was strong, and he knew that his hand was in Jannah (Heaven). He didn't lose his trust in Allah for a moment. In fact, his faith gave him hope for a brighter future.

Haytham's story isn't just about loss. It's about finding strength through faith when everything seems lost. While many of us would struggle to smile through such hardship, Haytham shows us what it means to truly trust in Allah. He knows his hand is in Jannah, and he has hope in Allah for a brighter future. This unshakeable faith is what makes Haytham truly remarkable. He may have lost his hand, but he gained something even more powerful—emaan that is unshakeable.

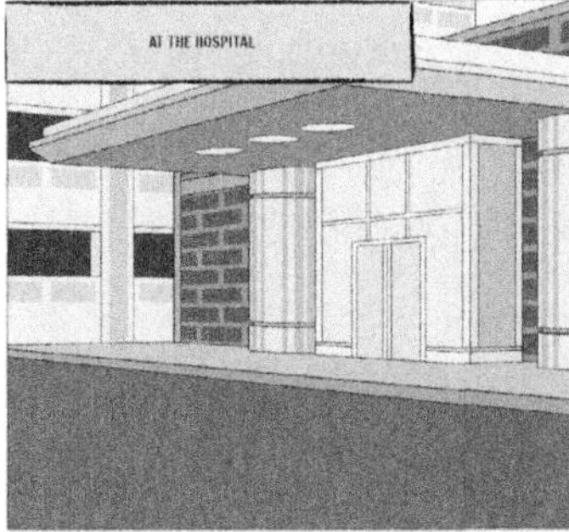


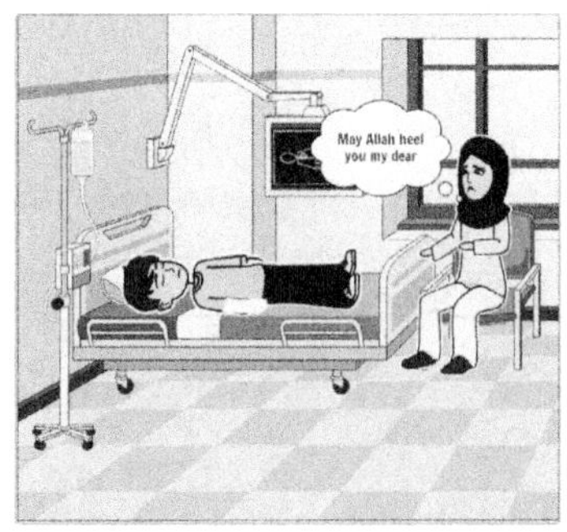

Based on a story originally reported by Al Jazeera Media Network., June 2024

Link: https://www.instagram.com/reel/C8q8dSPS8jP/

# A Culinary Comfort

By Muhammad Waabil

In the midst of Gaza's relentless turmoil, where the sounds of conflict overshadow the hopes of its people, one girl has found a beacon of light in an unexpected place—her kitchen. Renad, a ten-year-old girl whose love for cooking was awakened by the harsh reality of war, has turned her passion into a symbol of resilience, hope, and life.

Before the war, Renad's culinary skills were an unremarkable part of her life, an occasional indulgence in the art of cooking. But as the conflict escalated, her kitchen became her sanctuary—a space where she could momentarily escape the harsh realities surrounding her. The chaos outside may have taken much from her, but it ignited a passion within her that she had never known.

Renad's Instagram account, where she shares her culinary creations, has become a testament to her spirit. With over 520,000 followers, her platform serves as a source of inspiration to many. Each post—a vibrant snapshot of a meal, a recipe shared with warmth and hope—reflects not just her skill but her determination to spread joy amidst despair.

For Renad, food is more than sustenance. It is a distraction from the nightmares she has lived through and a way to reclaim a semblance of normalcy from the wreckage of her childhood. The dishes she prepares tell stories of tradition and comfort, a bridge between her past and an uncertain future. They echo the life she once knew and stand as a testament to her resilience.

The global community has rallied around Renad, offering support and encouragement. Yet, it is the unwavering backing of her family that provides the true foundation for her success. Behind every post and every recipe is a network of love and support, ensuring that her culinary endeavours continue despite the severe food insecurity that plagues Gaza.

Renad's story is a reminder of the power of the human spirit and creativity. In a world where darkness often overshadows light, her kitchen has become a place of refuge and hope. Through her passion for cooking, she not only brings joy to her followers but also fuels a broader message of perseverance and the enduring strength of the human heart.

As Gaza continues to face its challenges, Renad's journey offers a glimmer of hope. Her story, woven into the fabric of her daily life and shared with the world, stands as a symbol of the indomitable spirit of its people.

Based on a story originally reported by Al Jazeera Media Network, 30 Jun

Link: https://www.youtube.com/watch?v=ej_7zlkMFjk

# Defying All Odds

By Hameeda Kassim
Comic by Noor Fatima

Asif Abu Mhadi is his name. Eleven years old, and he's lost a limb. Despite these challenges, and the constant dangers of war, he refuses to give up on his dreams, and continues to fight against all odds.

Asif was born during a time of war, and has experienced many wars in Gaza. Before the current war going on, Asif was very passionate about playing football. He used to play for Al Wahda Football Academy, dreaming of scoring goals, and pursuing a career in the sport.

But one day, everything changed—his home was shelled in an Israeli air strike. When it happened, he didn't think it was real—he thought that he was dreaming. The roof of the house came crashing down, and it went totally dark, chaos erupting around him. His brother narrowly escaped death, a piece of shrapnel grazing his neck. Asif's brother carried him all the way to Al Awda hospital, despite the heavy shelling that continued relentlessly. Can you imagine how frightening that journey to the hospital would've been for both Asif and his brother? Sometimes, we avoid going out due to certain weather conditions, such as heavy rain—but this was not rain. Their lives were on the line, and instead of cool raindrops falling from the sky, instead there were raging bombs. Even getting hit by one would have destroyed them both.

From Al Awda, Asif was transferred to Al Aqsa hospital, where one of his legs was amputated and if that wasn't awful enough, the amputation was carried out without anaesthetics.

I'd like you to stop and think for a moment—if your leg was amputated, what would your initial reaction be? Would you not be sad due to the loss of your leg, and complaining about the circumstances? You might even be angry at the injustice of it all. Yet, even in the face of such overwhelming challenges, Asif did not ask, "Why me? Under what circumstances do I deserve what happened to me?" Instead of complaining, he remained grateful to God.

With a smile he said "Alhamdulillah" All praise and thanks belongs to Allah.

His injury did not flatten his spirit in the slightest. He is determined to reclaim his place on the football field, despite everything. He said that he will defy all odds, including his injury, and that he will continue to chase his dreams in football. The fact that he will require a prosthetic leg to play again is not nearly enough to stop him from achieving his heart's desire. Even when he was in hospital, he never lost hope of playing football again, and also returning to school to continue his education.

He could've let his injury shatter his dreams, and given up and given up as soon as life presented its hardships to him. Amazingly, he didn't.

What gave him such hope and courage, except for his trust in Allah (swt)! His trust in Allah had become his superpower giving him hope instead of sinking into despair.

He shared his dream to one day meet his favourite footballer and role model is Yassine

Bounou, who is the Moroccan national team's goalkeeper. Asif said, "I will go to him even with only one foot."

Little did he know, that this dream was about to come true!

Just a few days later, he received a video call from Yassine Bounou!

His heartfelt statement hadcaught the attention of many, going viral and eventually reaching Bounou himself, who responded by video calling Asif. The young boy was so overwhelmed with emotion that he could not hold back his tears of joy!

This story is a an inspiration to anyone who hears it. It is not only a story of survival—It is a story of a boy with trust in Allah(swt) which has become his power, allowing him to refuse to be defined by circumstances, to not give up and no matter what life throws at him. Ultimately, it is a story of hope in Allah (swt).

www.storyboardthat.com

StoryboardThat

I was transferred to Al Aqsa Hospital. where one of my legs was amputated - if that wasn't bad enough, the amputation was done WITHOUT any anesthetics

Yet even in the face of such overwhelming challenges, I was thankful to Allah

I used to play for Al Wahda Football Academy, and I am determined to reclaim I place on the field. I said that I will defy all odds, including my injury, and that I will continue to chase my dreams in football. The fact that I will require a prosthetic leg to play again is not nearly enough to stop me from achieving my heart's desire. Even when I was in hospital, I never lost hope of playing football again, and also returning to school to continue his education

My injury did not flatten my spirit in the slightest.
My Favourite FOOT BALLER IS YASSMIN BOUNOU Morocoon national team's goalkeeper.. I said, "I will go to him even with only one foot." This heartfelt statement caught the attention of many, going viral and eventually reaching Bounou myself , who responded by video calling me was so overwhelmed with emotion that he could not hold back I
tears.

Based on a story originally reported by Al Jazeera English, 20 Nov 2023

Links:

https://www.youtube.com/watch?v=Dlb-dk99seo

# Echoes of Hope

By Wajeeh uddin

In a small, war-torn village in Gaza, lives Yazan Fasfous, a brave thirteen-year-old boy. Before the war, Yazan's life was much like any other boy his age. He spent his days going to school, playing football with friends, and dreaming about the future. But when the war began, everything changed. The sound of explosions replaced the laughter of his friends, and the future he once dreamed of seemed far away. But instead of sitting in despair or thinking, "I'm just a kid, what can I do?" Yazan asked himself a different question: "What can I do to help?"

Rather than feeling helpless, Yazan decided to act. He saw the struggle around him, the pain and suffering, and he knew he had to do something. So he chose to volunteer alongside his mother at a local hospital. His mother, who works in the medical supplies department, became his guiding light during these dark times. For the past nine months, Yazan has been by her side, helping in any way he can.

The hospital is a place where hope and despair live side by side. Yazan's days are long and hard. He often works through the night, with little sleep. The weight of the situation is heavy, and the constant sound of sirens and distant explosions only adds to the stress. The urgency in the air leaves him no time to rest; as soon as one order of supplies is ready, another is needed. The pressure feels endless, and the chaos never stops. He misses the days when his biggest worry was finishing his homework or scoring a goal in a football game, but now, life has given him much greater challenges.

But Yazan finds strength in his purpose. He knows that every small act of kindness can make a difference, even in the face of so much adversity. Instead of whining or giving in to fear, he puts his energy into his work. The gratitude in the eyes of the people they help, the brief smiles of patients and their families, and the quiet moments of solidarity with his mother give him the courage to keep going. Even though the work is tough and the dangers are real, Yazan stays firm.

Yazan's dedication and courage grew stronger with each passing day. He realises that his work is more than just delivering supplies—it's about bringing hope to those who need it most. The small acts of kindness he offers become a source of light in a dark world. He understands that, even though he's just a boy, his actions can have a big impact. He learns that being young doesn't mean being powerless.

Through his journey, Yazan becomes more than just a helper at the hospital. He becomes a beacon of hope himself, shining brightly even in the shadow of war. His bravery and commitment show that even in the hardest times, one person can make a big difference. Yazan might have once been just a schoolboy with dreams of football, but now, he's a symbol of strength and resilience for his entire community. By choosing to ask "What CAN I do?" Instead of feeling helpless, Yazan has proven that even the smallest actions, driven by a big heart, can make the world a better place.

Based on a story originally reported by Al Jazeera Media Network., 10 Dec 2023

Link: https://youtu.be/laONrute8qg

# Lulu's Cries: Cats of Gaza, Comfort to Children

By Lucas Azmi Gallardo

In Gaza, an eight-year-old boy had a peaceful life with his cat, Lulu. Lulu was his best friend, always there to keep him company. Meanwhile, my cat, Lily, was afraid of simple things like vacuum cleaners. But Lulu's life was different. Instead of being scared of harmless noises, she had to face the terrifying sounds of bombs.

When the bombing started, the boy's world turned upside down. The loud explosions shook their home, and Lulu would hide with the boy's grandmother, trembling in fear. The war made everything uncertain, and the boy's family had to leave their home to stay safe. But even in the chaos, the boy couldn't forget about Lulu. She was too important to him. So, his family made a brave decision—they paid two hundred and fifty shekels to go back and save her. Lulu was precious to him, and he couldn't leave her behind.

As they moved to safety, the boy began to wonder about the difference between cats and people. He thought about how cats have feelings too, how they get hungry and thirsty just like we do. Lulu became his source of comfort. Whenever things got really scary, she would put a smile on his face. He knew Lulu was good to him, and he wanted to share that happiness. He let the other kids in their tent area play with Lulu to make them feel better too.

Life in the tents was hard. The boy's family often didn't have enough food, but they always made sure to save something for Lulu. They would share donations of canned food, meat, and cheese with her. Despite their struggles, the boy and his family found comfort in caring for Lulu. And it wasn't just them—many people in the camp felt the same way.

The true heart of the people of Palestine shines through in the story of Lulu and her young owner. Even in times of great hardship, when most would focus only on their own survival and their families, the people of Gaza still find room in their hearts to care for their animals. This gentleness and kindness, even amidst the harshest of circumstances, show the true spirit of the Palestinian people. They remind us that compassion doesn't fade in the face of adversity—it grows stronger.

Based on a story originally reported by A Middle East Eye., 9 Nov 2023
Link:
https://www.youtube.com/watch?v=k-7MkSPjAbE

# The Quran's Wisdom Through the Boy's Answer

By Hassan-Mustafa Khalifa

As he walked through the desolate streets, the destruction around him was overwhelming. Rubble was scattered everywhere, like stars fallen from a shattered sky over Palestine. The air was heavy with the acrid smell of smoke, blood and the sharp tang of burning metal. Dead bodies lay strewn across Gaza like crushed dolls abandoned in a forgotten world, families broken like fragile glass shattered by a sudden blow. Beloved memories lying demolished, reduced to fragments. Cries from war-torn buildings echoed around the streets like haunting wails of souls trapped. It was like a nightmare had infiltrated the real world.

The boy paused, taking in the full scope of the devastation. The once vibrant city now in ruins, bore the scars of years of relentless conflict. A man approached him, his eyes filled with questions. "How come Allah does not support us in Gaza even though we are upon the truth and the Jews are on falsehood?" he asked.

The boy, his faith unwavering, replied with words from the Qur'an. "And if Allah, praise and glory be to Him, had willed, He could have taken vengeance upon them Himself, but He tests some of you by means of others." Isn't it incredible how a young boy, who has known nothing but destruction for months can give such an answer?

The boy was asked again, "And these poor people who are dying, mistreated, and humiliated—how is it their fault?"

With calm conviction, the boy continued, "If we read the next verse, the Lord of the worlds says, 'And to those who are killed in the cause of Allah—never will he waste their deeds. He will guide them and amend their condition and admit them to Paradise, which he has made known to them.'" (Surah 47:4-6).

Despite the unimaginable suffering he endured, his faith remained unshaken. The boy's answer carried a sense of determination that transcended the immediate suffering. He persevered, refusing to be broken by the trials before him. His faith was like an ancient olive tree standing firm against a storm.

Remembering the footsteps of the Prophet (Peace be upon him) and his companions who faced immense hardships and emerged stronger, so too do the people of Palestine draw strength from their faith. Their resilience mirrors the courage of those who came before them, who, despite all obstacles, trusted in Allah's wisdom and guidance.

In every challenge, they find inspiration in the Prophet's journey, knowing that their suffering is not in vain. It is a path that has been walked before, and like the Prophet (PBUH) and his companions, they hold on to the belief that victory in this life or the next lies with Allah.

With a smile on his face, the boy continued forward, knowing that life in this world is temporary and that Allah is enough to lead him through the darkness.

The story of this boy and his people is not just one of suffering, but of enduring faith, hope, and an unshakable belief in something greater. And though they may face death, they do so with the hope that in Jannah, a better world awaits.

The people of Palestine young and old continue to find strength and solace in their faith even as the world around them crumbles, There is both pain and promise and a deep understanding that while their bodies may be vulnerable, their spirit is not and a belief that no matter how powerful the enemy, they are ultimately under the dominion of a higher power.

Based on a story originally reported on 20 Apr 2024
Link: https://www.instagram.com/reel/C5-HWL2Bj9o/

# Raza's fight: A Journey Beyond Pain

By Muhammad Novsarka

Based on a story originally reported by Al Jazeera Media Network., 2 Feb 2024

Link:
https://www.youtube.com/watch?v=WSoH34PYRh4

# Here We Shall Stay

By Hameeda Kassim

Samah Khalid Naji is an eighteen year old girl—she graduated form high school with a grade of ninety-four point six percent! She had only been to university for two weeks before the destruction of the war followed in October, and the life she once knew was snatched away without warning.

Samah is living in the ruins of her Gaza home. Her house was bombed in an Israeli air strike. When her house was bombed, Samah's father, Khalid Saeed Naji, age fifty-one was in the house along with Samah's mother and brother. Her father was injured in his arms, chest, and mouth—this led to him getting stitches done in his mouth and him being unable to close his fingers into a fist.

Even sharing this story can bring tears to one's eyes—so just imagine experiencing it firsthand.

Samah wanted to calm down and reassure her younger siblings, and be strong but when she saw the state her father was in, she couldn't stop herself from crying. Samah could hardly believe the level of destruction her home faced. She would never have expected everything she knew to be reduced to rubble.

Samah's family sought shelter in al Aqsa hospital, thinking that it would be a safe harbour for them, and a place where the Israeli would not strike. They set up a tent there, but soon realised they would not be safe from shrapnel or rocks that would come from any potential missile strikes. So, although her family's home was destroyed, they returned. They thought it would be safer there, close to al Aqsa, but also in their own space, as a family. Khalid stated that he built their house himself, brick by brick. He used to mix the cement himself, and sometimes Khalid's wife would come to help him.

Samah said that her dad means everything to her, and that if it wasn't for him, her life would be very different. She said that her dad is the kindest person that she knows, and that if he did not survive, she and her family surely would have not been able to continue.

Khalid and his family could've complained, and said "Why is this happening to us? What did we do to deserve this?"

But, Khalid told a neighbour that he could hardly believe he survived the bombing. He thought of other families that were killed and torn apart in their own homes, and said that his family got off lightly by the grace of God. Although they had lost their house, that can be rebuilt. But if a family is torn apart, the scars of the past will take much, much longer to heal.

When the house was hit, the family's cat which they have had for seven years was inside. They assumed that she ran away from the destruction and chaos, and clung to the hope that she survived. A week after the bombing, Khalid was passing the house to inspect it, and

I think you can guess what he came across—their cat!

She ran after Khalid as if she was calling out to him. The cat made Samah's siblings, Yousef and Layan overjoyed. It was a small victory after all the losses they've faced, and the harrowing things they've experienced. With their cat's return, it made the weight of the world on their shoulders lessen slightly.

Yousef said that when he looks around the ruins of his house, he feels like he is surrounded by ghosts. That constant feeling of knowing that your home is gone, completely and utterly destroyed without any means of reversal is heartbreaking.

In their home, they had an area where lush plants and flowers grew, adding colour to their home—they had lemons, figs, guava, mloukhia, peppers, basil, cactuses, and more—Samah said it was the most beautiful space they had, and it was calming. But the airstrike reduced everything to ash, and now there is nothing calming about that area in their house anymore.

Samah stated that every single centimetre of Gaza is dangerous. Each one of the people in Gaza have been trying to reach out to the world, and trying to send messages to us all. Not once in the video did Samah or any of her family members say a single word of hatred towards the Israeli forces—that isn't the intention behind this story. What Samah, and other people like her all over Gaza want is for the world to listen. But instead of answering their call for help, we turn away, and do nothing. Samah wrote messages on the walls in her spare time when she didn't know what else to occupy herself with. She wrote "*Where is my home? Where is humanity? All we wish for is to return to our previous life that we complained about, but we can't.*" All she wants is the life she used to consider boring. The life where she didn't have to worry about bombs dropping out of the sky, the life where her home was still intact—the life where peace was a right, and not a privilege.

Based on a story originally reported by Al Jazeera Media Network., 24 Jan 2024

# Who Has the Power?

Comic and Story by Maha Tola

"Israel may have better weaponry than we do, but we have Allah. He is more powerful."

Those were the wise words of a boy who is currently in the destruction of palestine. But this story might not be as depressing as it seems.

Obviously this war is a huge problem—but while we might not be able to stop this war completely, the least we can do is try to help. The boy said, *"All the planes coming to us can't harm us. Their planes and drones over us, but they are beneath Allah's throne. And that's why we have Allah who is above them."*

How beautiful is it, that they are still thinking on the bright side no matter what happens? No matter what they do to the Palestinian people, they will always stay strong. "We shall continue to stand even if the whole world is against us. This soul, if we die as martyrs, is Allah's. Yes, seeing martyrs getting injured hurts, but we should also keep Allah's teachings in mind."

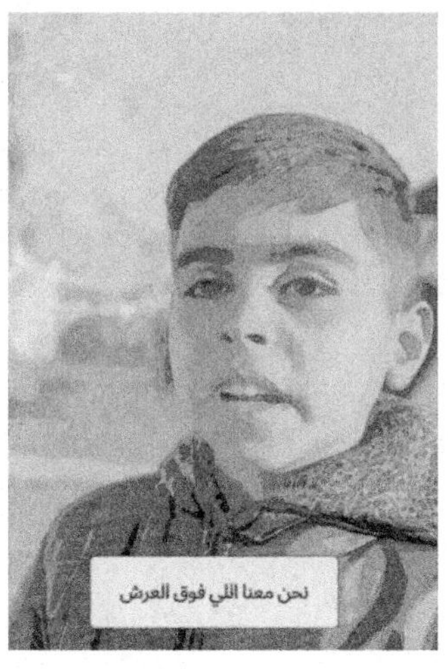


*"Do not falter in pursuit of the enemy—if you are suffering, they too are suffering. But you can hope to receive from Allah what they can never hope for. And Allah is all-knowing, all wise." Quran*

The people of Palestine, still remain strong even after all this trouble, and although they might die on this earth, a reward may await them in Jannah.

I am Mahmud. My older sister is Kawthar. We are among the orphans of Palestine.

Everyday, we live in hiding, scared. We have to walk for miles just to get little food and

We don't have much clothes or clean things to use.

We live in a small
house and wish
for a better life.

BEFORE ISRAEL ATTACKS RAFAH............

I think I see home! Alhamdulillah! I'm starving!
Hey Mahmud!
Zakaria! I gotta go right now! We'll talk later InshAllah!

Assalamualaikum!

So, how was school?
Good Allahamdulliah!
After you eat, can you go buy some bread?
Of course, InshAllah!

Just paying for these?
Yes. Thank you.

What's that sound? Its sounds like its close to my home!
EEEEEEE EEEEEEE E!

My home is all gone.....And so is my Mother!

Link: https://www.instagram.com/reel/C8E2TfhA4yL/

# Faith In The Air

By Zara Shaheen

In Gaza, a place known for its beauty and lively spirit, there are many amazing people who have strong faith, even when things are really tough. One man there had a story that is both touching and inspiring.

During a time of great difficulty, with the sound of war all around, someone asked this man, "How will you keep going after all this destruction, you no food, no water, no fuel ?"

With a calmness that seemed to rise above the chaos, the man answered, "Allah is here. There is no problem. He has a plan. He is the provider."

Think about how deep this answer is. In a place where so many people have died, jobs have been lost, and homes have been destroyed, this man's faith is still strong. His belief in a bigger plan and divine support is like a light in the darkness.

This reminds us how easy it is to forget our own blessings when we face our own problems. Seeing someone hold onto their faith in such hard times makes us think about our own lives and how we handle challenges.

Stories like these open our eyes and help us see and appreciate the good things in our lives, even if they seem small. They show us that even in the hardest times, faith and hope can guide us. May this man's strong belief remind us of the power of faith and the amazing strength of the human spirit.

Based on a story originally reported on 23 Dec 2023

# On Their Own

By Inara Sidra

In Gaza, 13-year-old Mohammad Al Yazji lived an ordinary life with his parents and eight younger siblings—Mayer, Toleen, Youssef, Sewar, Zaher, Wared, Fatima, and Mayse. Like most teens, Mohammad didn't know how to care for babies or manage a household; his mother handled everything. But when war erupted, his world was turned upside down. Three days after the conflict began, Mohammad's mother rushed out to check on her parents, only to be killed in an airstrike.

With their mother gone and their father missing, Mohammad was thrust into a position no child should face—he had to become both the father and mother to his siblings. He had no time to grieve or process the loss; survival was the priority. Mohammad, once a carefree teenager, now had to take on a great responsibility.

His youngest sister, Toleen, was a particular challenge for Mohammad because she cried most of the time, and he didn't know much about how to care for her. He fed her and put her to sleep every day, but he felt lost without his mother's guidance. Each day was a struggle.

Every morning, Mohammad wakes up early, searching for water, gathering firewood, and ensuring his siblings are fed. The tasks are overwhelming, but he knows he can't give up. The fear and uncertainty are constant as bombs continue to fall. His youngest sister, Toleen, becomes ill and has to be taken to the hospital, adding to Mohammad's burden. The challenges are immense, and he feels the weight of responsibility like never before

.

Despite these hardships, Mohammad's determination never wavers. He dreams of bringing some joy to his siblings, imagining the day he can buy them a soccer ball so they can forget the horrors of war, even if just for a moment. The kindness of neighbors offers some relief, providing food and supplies, but it's Mohammad's unwavering strength that keeps the family together.

Though Mohammad is just 13, instead of whining or giving in to despair, he draws upon his deep faith in Allah to rise to the moment. He embraces the responsibility of caring for his siblings, proving that strength and maturity are not defined by age. Mohammad emerges as a true hero, showing incredible courage and resilience in the face of unimaginable adversity. He has learned to protect his family and to find hope where there seems to be none. For Mohammad, the journey is far from over, but he faces the future with the knowledge that he can endure whatever comes their way, as long as they have each other and their faith.

Based on a story originally reported by NBC News., 20 Jan 2024
Link:
https://www.youtube.com/watch?v=E2vfdbLz9zk

# The Palestinian Newton

By Zubair Ahmad

In the heart of Gaza, resides a bright young boy named Hossam Al Atta, whose genius has brought light to his family's home in a unique way. Hossam, with his unwavering determination and creative spirit,came up with a brilliant solution to tackle the frequent power outages that were in his community.

To solve the electricity problem, Hossam bought a dynamo. Knowing he needed to turn it to generate electricity, he cleverly used a fan to do the job. When the wind blew, it provided even more electricity.

Through this genius idea, Hossam successfully harnessed the power of movement to generate electricity, providing his family with a reliable source of light amidst the darkness. How inspiring is it that even in all the destruction, Hossam still managed to find a source of light even though all they've known is the dark?

Hossam Al Atta, the bright young boy from Gaza who brought light to his family's home, is now dreaming even bigger. He wants to find a way to power up the entire camp and provide electricity to everyone living there. With his creative mind and determination, Hossam has already started working on ideas to make this dream come true.

But the situation in Gaza is tough. Diseases are spreading, especially among children. Sadly, Hossam became very sick before he could achieve his goal. Despite this setback, his spirit remains strong. Hossam's story is a powerful reminder of resilience and hope. We pray that Allah (swt) cures him and grants him even greater ideas to help his community.

Hossam Al Atta's story shows how even a child can make a big difference using creativity and intelligence. He found a way to bring light to his family's home, proving that you don't have to be an adult to solve problems. Hossam's efforts inspire us all, reminding us that anyone, no matter how young, can use their ideas to help others. His journey is a powerful example of how one person's determination can bring hope to many.

Based on a story originally reported by Al Jazeera Media Network.,5 Feb 2024
Link:
https://www.youtube.com/watch?v=dmB3mwsJl-4&t=1s

# A Story of Little Nana

By Aaliyan Umair

Little Nana, a 7-year-old girl, ran to me, her Baba, as she always did for comfort and safety. But with the loud noises and flashes in the sky, which felt like a frightening dream, the once-familiar warmth of our neighbourhood became unsettling. When a blinding light filled the sky, we all fell to the ground, huddling together. Amidst our breaths and whispered fears, Nana told me, "I love you, Baba."

The world around us was chaotic, filled with the scent of smoke. In the dark, as I held my little girl, she tried to be brave, her voice trembling as she said, "Baba, I'm not afraid, just nervous!" I embraced her tightly, feeling her warmth, as if we were one. My feeling of helplessness was overwhelming. All I wanted in that moment was to keep her safe.

After a round of intense bombing, Nana drew a picture. It showed a house, a garden, a bright sun, and a sky clear of any threats. She chose not to draw birds, wanting the sky to be peaceful, but she did include clouds. Perhaps she was even a little wary of birds now.

She excitedly shared her plans, saying, "If we stay safe, we'll always be together and go to Aunt's and Grandpa's house." Little did she know that her aunt's house had been lost and her grandfather's home, with all its cherished memories and warmth, had turned to rubble.

I tried to be strong for the family, but I found myself crying several times. We cried together, sharing our grief for what we had lost and what we were experiencing. We didn't dwell on the future because we weren't sure what it held, but we found comfort in being together and holding onto hope.

*After a wave of violent bombing, 7-year-old Nana drew this picture, in which there is a house, a garden, a sweet sun and a clear sky free of swarms.*

Based on a story originally reported by Save the Children, 2024

Link:*https://www.savethechildren.org/us/charity-stories/child-story-from-gaza*

# Whispers of Hope

By Abeera Abbasi

Lama, a young journalist from Gaza, stood amidst the ruins of her childhood home, a place where her family had lived for generations. The house was gone, bombed into oblivion, like so many others in the city. As Lama sifted through the debris, she found fragments of memories—photographs, pieces of furniture, and other remains of a life that once was. "This is the hijab Auntie gave to me! You know the one who was martyred."

Despite the destruction, Lama's spirit remained undaunted. With each step through the rubble, Lama narrated the devastation that had befallen Gaza. The Israeli forces had not only targeted homes but had also left schools and hospitals in ruins, reducing everything to dust. The streets, once filled with the laughter of children and the hustle of daily life, were now eerily silent, marked only by destruction. Yet, as Lama walked past what remained of her old school, she thought about the resilience of the students who would one day return to rebuild their dreams.

Lama's heart ached as she spoke of the relentless bombing campaign that had left her city unrecognisable. She knew she had a duty to tell the world what was happening, to share the stories of those who no longer had a voice. Despite the overwhelming loss, Lama's resolve remained strong. She was determined to continue her work as a journalist, to document the truth, and to make sure the world did not forget Gaza and its people. With a hopeful glimmer in her eye, she vowed to capture not only the pain but also the enduring spirit of her city and its people.

Based on a story originally reported by Al Jazeera Media Network., 19 Mar 2024

Link:*https://www.aljazeera.com/program/newsfeed/2024/3/19/aspiring-journalist-lama-visits-her-destroyed-home-in-gaza*

# The Paper Plane Kid

By Khizer

In a town scarred by conflict, where the sky was often filled with more than just clouds, a young boy found a way to bring a touch of hope to those around him. The sounds of war echoed through the streets, but amidst the destruction, he found comfort in something simple: paper planes.

Every day, the boy would gather scraps of paper—old newspapers, discarded flyers, anything that could be folded. His hands, small but steady, would transform these seemingly useless scraps into delicate planes. They weren't just toys; they were symbols of resilience, and hope.

This young boy decided to bring smiles on the faces of other children who had lost their homes, their toys, their family.

In the late afternoon, when the sun began to dip and shadows grew long, the boy would set out to the remnants of the marketplace.

Despite the danger, he made a stall of paper airplanes and paper toys for kids.

And the boy would, running home with the paper clutched tightly in his hands, ready to make more planes.

But for now, his planes were made of paper, fragile and light, just like the lives of the children who played with them. Yet in their fragility, there was a quiet strength. Each plane that took flight was a small act of defiance, a reminder that even in the darkest times, hope could still rise.

Each plane that soared into the sky carried with it the collective hopes of a generation of children who had known nothing but war.

Based on a story originally reported by Middle East Eye., 20 Mar 2024
Link:
https://www.youtube.com/watch?v=X0yhrhNnrPE

# Rahaf's Wishes

By Nurkamila Safia

Once, a ten-year-old girl named Rahaf lived in Gaza City, surrounded by family and friends. But life in Gaza had become dangerous, and one day, Rahaf and her family were told by the IDF to flee south, where they promised it would be safe. Holding on to hope, they packed up and left their home. Yet, as they traveled, the sound of bombs filled the air, shaking their hearts with fear. Rahaf's mother prayed continuously, seeking protection as they moved forward, unsure of what lay ahead.

Their journey was filled with terror. Along the way, Zionist soldiers stopped them, their presence intimidating and cold. One by one, the soldiers called out the travelers, forcing them to pass under tanks. The family prayed, reciting Al-Ikhlas ten times from the Qur'an, hoping for heaven if this was their final moment. Their faith gave them strength as they faced the unknown.

It was Rahaf's birthday, the 11th of November, but it didn't feel like a celebration. She saw the soldiers up close, her heart pounding. She began to cry, fearing the worst. The soldiers took a young man from their group and made him strip. They warned him, "If you don't come to us, none of them will pass." Helpless, the man complied and was taken captive. Then, they seized another person, and his fate remained a mystery. The third was a disabled man. His mother pleaded, "He cannot speak; he is disabled!" But the soldiers didn't listen. When the mother begged to go with her son, they refused. Her tears and cries fell on deaf ears, and eventually, the soldiers allowed the rest to pass.

Despite the constant danger, Rahaf wished for peace. On her birthday, instead of gifts, she silently wished for the war to end, for the bombings to stop. But the violence continued. Her two-year-old brother was injured in a bombing, the fire from the explosion burning him. It was nighttime when the screams of her brother woke the family, their hearts racing with fear for his safety.

Meanwhile, Rahaf's grandfather, who depended on kidney dialysis, stopped receiving treatment. Whether he was still alive or not was unknown to them. Their family was torn apart by the war. Rahaf's school, once a place of learning and joy, had been bombed, and her principal, a person she admired, was killed. She missed her friends, her school, and the life she once knew.

Through all this pain, Rahaf's family held on to their courage. Her mother, preparing for the worst, had asked all of her daughters to write a will, a heartbreaking reminder of their daily reality. Rahaf, still just a child, wrote hers too. She asked her sisters to take care of their parents and her little brother if something happened to her. She even asked how she wanted to be buried.

Yet, in the midst of this unimaginable hardship, Rahaf's story is not just one of loss. It is a story of resilience, of holding on to faith when the world seems to crumble around you. Even as the bombs fell, Rahaf and her family prayed, holding tight to the belief that better days would come. Her journey shows us that even in the darkest of times, hope and courage can survive.

Source: Based on a story originally reported by falastiniyat, 24 Dec 2023
Link:
https://padlet.com/emaanpowerteam/remake-of-palestine-videos-9lr4xerh8q2reqst/wish/j40PQDB6lbReWvXB

# The Gaza Man

By Ahmed Ahmed

Mohammed Khamis Hamada's journey is a testament to the resilience of the human spirit. At just 18, he became the first Olympic weightlifter for Palestine at the Tokyo 2020 Olympics, bringing hope to a nation despite its drastic state. Weightlifting is a family legacy, with his older brother, Hussam, serving as both his coach and inspiration.

Life in Gaza is a constant struggle. Amid relentless conflict and devastating bombings, Mohammed and his family faced unimaginable hardships. Despite the chaos and uncertainty, his determination to succeed never wavered. The streets of Gaza, marked by destruction and loss, were his training ground. With resources scarce and the constant threat of violence, Mohammed pushed forward, driven by a desire to bring recognition to his country through his sport.

The decision to leave Gaza in 2022 was fraught with heartache. Hussam had to make the agonising choice to leave his wife and three young children behind, unsure of their safety or when they would be reunited. In Gaza, food was a challenge to get due to the high expense after the bombing, and they often relied on animal feed to survive. The weight of leaving his family in such dire conditions was a heavy burden, yet the pursuit of their Olympic dream demanded this sacrifice.

Despite facing setbacks, including a temporary suspension due to counterfeit supplements that he had taken without knowing, Mohammed's spirit remained unbroken. In Norway, as he prepared for a tournament, the toll of the war and malnutrition was evident. He had lost over 18 kilograms and could only lift a fraction of his previous weight. Yet, his resolve never faltered.

The Olympic authorities recognized his extraordinary circumstances and considered granting him an exception for the 2024 Olympics. Even though his name was not on the final list, Mohammed's dedication and perseverance shone through.

Now, with his sights set on the 2028 Olympics in Los Angeles, Mohammed continues to train with unwavering commitment. His story is one of courage and determination, a beacon of hope for his people. Mohammed Khamis Hamada is not just lifting weights; he is lifting the dreams of an entire nation, proving that even in the darkest times, the human spirit can rise above adversity.

Source: Based on a story originally reported by Al Jazeera., 11 Aug 2024

Link: https://www.youtube.com/watch?v=eFJd5f1-fGw

# Straightforward Duty

By Sabriyah Idris

In Deir Al Balah, a small tent stood on the dusty ground, surrounded by ruins. The sky was often gray, filled with smoke, and the once-green fields were now just patches of dry earth. Inside the tent lived Maha Al Sarsak, a fifteen-year-old girl with the weight of the world on her young shoulders.

Within the chaos of survival, this a fifteen-year-old girl lives with her 8 little siblings and a hardworking mom in the tents of Gaza.. She is very diligent, yet dutiful towards her family. Not many young ladies have much work to do, but this one does many different chores.

Every morning, before the sun had a chance to warm the chilly air, Maha would wake up. Her hands, once soft, had become rough and calloused from washing clothes every day. It wasn't much, but

With such a large family each sibling has to be taken care of with patience. The girl is the eldest in the family so most of the tasks rely on her to complete such as travelling long distances to get water using her bare hands to wash untidy clothes, cleaning the dirty floors with no equipment other than a fragmented rake, just to earn a little money for her family to survive.

Many of these problems are disliked by her. But even so she still works hard everyday having faith because she knows that there is something better that's waiting for her in the end.

Source: Based on a story originally reported by Al Jazeera., 9 Aug 2024

Link:
https://www.youtube.com/watch?v=UCILf1kf4el&t=8s

# The Small Boy

By Faryal Ismail

In the shattered land of Palestine, a small boy, no older than ten, wandered the broken streets, clutching a basket filled with freshly baked pizza. The sun beat down mercilessly, but the boy's determination drove him forward. Each day, he walked these streets, hoping to sell enough food to bring a few shekels home, enough to help his family survive.

He spent hours walking back and forth, his small feet aching with every step, yet he refused to give up. Even as the sun began to set, casting long shadows over the ruins, the boy clung to hope.

One day, while walking across the demolished streets with his now slightly cooled but still scrumptious pizza, the boy came across a very tall man. The man knelt to meet the boy's eyes, his face soft with concern. "What are you selling?" the man asked gently.

The boy, awed by the kindness in the stranger's voice, replied eagerly, "Pizza. Buy from me please!"

The man smiled warmly and asked, "How much does one cost?"

The boy hesitated, calculating in his head, trying to remember what his mother taught him about prices and fairness. After a few moments, he responded, "Seven shekels for all of them.'"

As the boy spoke, the man began asking him about his family. The boy's gaze dropped to the ground as he explained, "We don't have much money... So, I try to help by selling food. My mother makes the pizzas, and I go out to sell them."

The man listened intently, his heart aching for the boy's struggle. He then reached into his pocket and pulled out 100 shekels, placed them gently into the boy's trembling hands. "This is for you," the man said softly. "You've worked so hard. Keep the pizzas and take this home to your family."

The boy stared at the money, his heart racing with a mix of confusion, disbelief, and overwhelming gratitude. Shocked and unable to speak, the boy smiled softly.

The man smiled as well, a gentle, reassuring smile, and said, "Sometimes, we all need a little help. And your hard work deserves to be recognized. Go home, rest, and tell your mother thank you for the delicious pizza."

Just a few months ago, this young boy perhaps used to go to school and his mom would make him pizza for lunch. But today, he is walking with a tray of pizza in rags, in the hot streets of

Gaza, hoping to earn a shekel by selling his mother's pizzas, so they can survive.

Source: Based on a story originally reported on 15 May 2024
Link: https://www.youtube.com/shorts/XxJE-_QrG1U

# Garden of Light

By Nana-Asmaou Shareef

In Gaza, where daily life can be very difficult, an inspiring act of faith and strength is taking place. Six young girls from this troubled area came together in a simple tent mosque to recite the entire Qur'an from memory in one sitting.

This impressive event was recorded in a video that went viral. Gaza, a small coastal area in Palestine, has faced harsh Israeli occupation for a long time.

With broken buildings, few resources, and the constant threat of violence, the children of Gaza face challenges that would be hard for anyone to handle. Despite these tough conditions, these six girls have shown resilience, which is a core value in Islam. They express the belief, "Indeed we belong to Allah and to Him we shall return."

This special moment happened when the girls, from young children to teenagers, gathered in the tent mosque to begin their recitation of the

Qur'an, which holds great significance. As the Prophet Muhammad (peace and blessings upon him) said:

*"No people gather together in one of the Houses of Allah, reciting the Book of Allah and studying it among themselves, except that Sakeenah (Tranquility) descends upon them, and Mercy envelops them, and the angels surround them, and Allah mentions them amongst those who are with him".*

As the sun rose over the damaged streets of Gaza, the girls, dressed in traditional Muslim clothing, took their places in the makeshift mosque. The excitement was clear as women of all ages gathered, eager to witness this impressive act of devotion.

With strong focus and discipline, the girls started their recitation, their voices moving together beautifully as they read the complex verses of the holy text. Even with the intense heat, which reached over 35°C (95°F) in the tent, the girls continued, shifting their positions and the people they were reciting to, determined to finish their task. Allah says:

*"Surely those who recite the Book of Allah, establish prayer and donate from what We have provided for them—secretly and openly—'can' hope for an exchange that will never fail * so that He will reward them in full and increase them out of His grace. He is truly All-Forgiving, Most Appreciative}*
(35:28)

The recitation of the Qur'an, the holy book of Islam, is very important for Muslims everywhere. Each letter recited brings great rewards in this life and the next. Memorising and reciting the entire text, which has over 6,000 verses, is seen as a significant act of devotion, a privilege and honour from Allah. Those who memorise it help pass down the Qur'an through generations.

Since October 7th, it has been reported that over 1,000 people in Gaza have memorised the Holy book. Their dedication is their greatest strength and protection.

For the girls in Gaza, this recitation was more than just showing their skills; it was a personal and spiritual journey. As the video spreads and reaches more people, we hope the story of these remarkable young women will inspire others to pursue their own spiritual goals, strengthen their connection with Allah, and explore the Qur'an to find its valuable teachings, becoming a source of light for others.

Source: Based on a story originally reported by IlmFeed., 24 Jun 2024
Link:
https://youtu.be/P7ZZbNO1-LE?si=wLMLZxbzL1hJNUUW

# Steps of Courage: Doha's Journey

By: Fatima Abbasi

In a world shattered by loss, how does a young girl find the strength to dream again? Doha is a 9-year-old bright little girl from Gaza. Once surrounded by the warmth of family and the comfort of home, her life was forever altered, one December evening when an airstrike reduced her house to rubble. In that tragic moment, she lost her parents and her sense of safety, but miraculously, Doha survived.

When she awoke in a hospital, her body bore the scars of the attack, including a severe leg injury that would forever limit her movements, making an already difficult life even more challenging. Yet, despite the overwhelming loss of her home, her parents, and her friends, Doha's spirit remains unbroken. She still dreams.

She dreams of becoming a physical therapist, using her own experience with pain to help others who suffer as she does. She dreams of returning to school once the war ends, of running and playing with friends in a time of peace. Though she has lost so much, she holds onto her dreams with a determination that defies her circumstances.

Now living with her grandparents in Rafah, Doha is piecing her life back together, day by day. Her resilience is an inspiration, a reminder that even in the face of unimaginable loss, the ability to dream endures. Many of us allow our dreams to be shattered by a single setback, but this little girl, who has lost everything and is still healing, dreams not only for herself but for others as well.

Source: Based on a story originally reported by UNICEF, 30 April 2024

Link:

https://www.unicef.org/sop/stories/dohas-brave-journey-loss-healing-gaza

# 11 Year Old Reporter

By Zainab Ahmad

A palestinian child. Sumayya Wushah, an 11 year old girl who is currently living through the war. Childhood. When you think of childhood you immediately think of the best years of my life. Your childhood where you spread your wings and fly freely. When you grow you develop a personality, some people are funny, some empathetic and some, well, are broken. Sumayya Wushah wouldn't want to be remembered as broken. She was strong, resilient and independant. A shield to her siblings, the moon amidst the dark night.

Inspired by the the journalist , she decided to become one herself, despite her young age and share with the world the suffering of her people.

She reports daily from the rubble filled streets in Gaza..

"This is the house where 17 people were martyred. Now I am standing next to Al-Sofara bakery. The only oven in Nuseirat which is functional. As we can see, many people are standing in line for a slice of bread", she reports among the ruins./ CNA

Source: Based on a story originally reported by CNA Media Company, 28 Feb 2024
Link:
https://www.cna.al/english/kosova-bota/vogelushja-11-vjecare-sfidon-friken-raporton-live-nga-lufta-ne-gaza-i391249

# The People of Palestine

by Mustafa

The People of Palestine

It is a bright sunny day. It is first day at school in Qatar. The teacher welcomes the kids and ensure they know each other.

The kids see each other and begin to introduce.

Fatima gets nervous as she is next to introduce herself.

Fatima makes up her mind and starts to introduce herself. Kids become curious seeing she has come from a situation different from them.

Now Fatima is touched and she begins to describe her homeland.

**As she continues she already begins to miss and scene her homeland. She takes pride explaining the prominent and distinct features of Palestinian culture.**

**She goes on.**

She explains the importance of Al-Aqsa mosque.

She is sadden by the situation

Everyone makes dua for Palestine.

Everyone tries to console her.

Source: Based on a story originally reported by Al Jazeera., 18 Nov 2023
Link:
https://www.aljazeera.com/gallery/2023/11/18/palestinian-wounded-children-evacuated-from-gaza-to-uae

# The Youngest Nurse in Gaza

By Adam Muhammad

How many twelve year olds do you find working at hospitals? It is not a common or even normal thing to have a child working at a hospital. However, since his family was displaced from the war on Gaza, twelve year old Zakaria Mohammad Salem Sarsak has been diligently volunteering at Al-Aqsa hospital. He does things that other twelve year olds don't ever have to do, like taking the injured to get x rays and scans and bringing the bodies of martyrs to the hospital morgue. All of these types of things are not only brave for Zakaria to do but they also extremely valuable contribution in time of need for his community.

Zakaria does a variety of tasks at Al-Aqsa. He transports patients and martyrs. He also distributes medicine to people who need it. He takes blood pressure readings and attaches IV to patients. Zakaria gets in his blue scrubs and dashes around the hospital, where he comforts and helps whoever and wherever he can. He watches over the patients and transports medical supplies through the hospital. Zakaria says that he learned most of what he knows from watching the doctors. Not only does Zakaria volunteer at Al-Aqsa hospital, he also travels with ambulances to sites of destruction and bombing to bring the injured and the dead back. It is incredible what the youngest worker at Al Aqsa is able to accomplish.

It is undoubtedly hard for a twelve year old to witness all that Zakaria has witnessed. His desire to volunteer is a reflection of his humanity and kindness. Deciding to be one of Gaza's youngest nurses is a very courageous thing to do after he and his whole family was displaced from his home. Zakaria says that he would rather play games with his brothers and friends, but "no longer has that option."

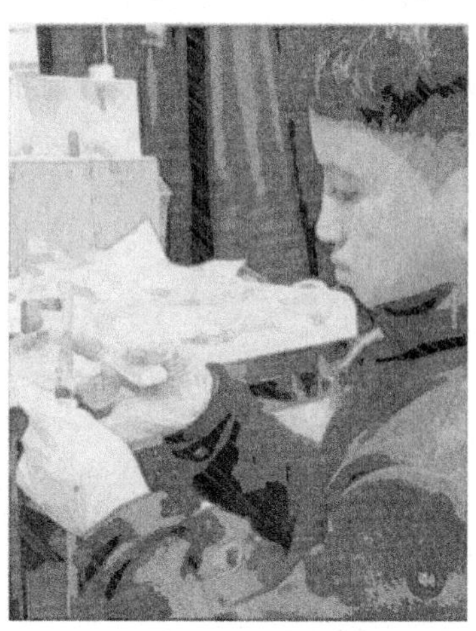

Zakaria's story at Al Aqsa hospital aired four months ago (April 2024) and has not been updated since. Al Aqsa was repeatedly bombed since then and his whereabouts are unknown. May Allah SWT protect him and his family and may we continue to be inspired by brave young Muslims like him.

Source: Based on a story originally reported by TRT World, 30 March 2024
Link:
https://www.youtube.com/watch?v=9O6tNxtgdvM

# Animals Also Matter

By Hanna Sophia

Lulu is a cat. It lives in West Gaza. With the on-going war, Lulu and the other animals are suffering too.

They are starving, hurt and scared. They get shelter and help from the people in Gaza. The people in Gaza are nice to Lulu.

Prophet Muhammad s.a.w. teach us to be kind to animals and all living things.

This shows that it is not only human in Gaza that are being hurt but also animals and all living things there. This should not be the case in life, we should not be treated just as numbers.

Based on a story originally reported by A Middle East Eye., 9 Nov 2023

Link:
https://www.youtube.com/watch?v=k-7MkSPjAbE

# Flicker of Hope

By: Hamzah Ansari

This is the story of an 11-year-old boy who loves creating inventions for fun. He walks home with two large bottles of water for his family. Before the war, he loved to create something out of nothing. The people of the camp nicknamed him the Newton of Gaza for his inventive spirit. He even created a wireless lock. His latest invention was a fan that works with wind power, channeling energy into the tent.

As he walks, he passes decomposing bodies on the street, feeling as if he's in a ghost town. The sight is extremely frightening because what happened to them could happen to him and his family. At night, he sleeps in fear, covering his face and closing his ears tightly to block out the sound of shelling. The constant threat of shrapnel hitting the tent and setting it on fire while they sleep is ever-present. Fear slowly wears away at a person's psyche, like a slow death.

He recently went to the doctor and was informed that he has hepatitis due to the food he ate. Before he got sick, he dreamed of lighting up the entire camp where he lives. Despite his illness, he remains determined. He vows to carry on once his health improves and complete his project, hoping to alleviate the suffering of the people in the camp. This determination shows the strength of faith the Palestinians hold.

Source: Based on a story originally reported by Al Jazeera, 5 February 2024

Link:
https://www.youtube.com/watch?v=dmB3mwsJI-4&t=1s

# The Wind of Palestine

A short story poem by Zainab Ahmad

Wind blowing down the streets of Gaza,
Rubble scattered round and round.
The sound of a janaza.
Amira walks with the wind,
Slowly and gracefully.
Her mother passed months ago.
Her father not too long ago.
But still it does not stop the sorrow,
Amira faces day by day,
Her heart hurts to hear the words they say.
Where was Shafique's janaza,
Was it in the streets of Gaza?
Stop. Stop the words.
Stop the killing.
In my head it's like a drilling,
It goes deeper and deeper,
Its okay though,
I pray,
Day by day,
I pray for the people of Palestine.
In Gaza,
I hope one day there will be no more.
Not one janaza.
But how can I be so certain,

When the blood around me is like a curtain.
Blinding all the light that shines through,
A segment of hope.
I need to cherish it.
Climb it like a rope.
Hold on for my life,
Every step I wobble and stumble.
I clutch my stomach as it begins to rumble.
Maybe I'm the rope of hope.
For the people of Palestine.
For the people of Gaza.
No more janaza.

# Echoes of the Olive Trees

A poem by Zaynab Shakoor

In the land where olive trees sway,
Where ancient stones whisper tales,
Palestine's heart beats every day,
Through valleys, hills, and trails.

A land of history, rich and deep,
Where cultures blend and meet,
Yet shadows cast a sorrowful sweep,
Where peace and conflict greet.

Children's laughter, dreams so bright,
In streets where hope is born,
Yet tears fall in the quiet night,
For lives and homes are torn.

Through struggles, voices rise and sing,
For justice, love, and peace,
In every heart, a hopeful spring,
For all the pain to cease.

Palestine, your spirit strong,
Through every trial and test,
May peace and freedom be your song,
And may you find your rest.

# Last Words

*O Allah, Protector of the oppressed, we ask You to safeguard the people of Palestine. Grant them security and peace, protect them from harm, and shield them from the cruelty of their oppressors. Cover them with Your mercy and protect their homes, families, and children. Ameen.*

As you close this book, we ask that you help amplify the voices of the children of Palestine by sharing "Voices from the olive trees" with others. Their stories of resilience, hope, and courage deserve to be heard far and wide. By sharing this book, you're not only spreading awareness but also standing in solidarity with the people of Palestine. Let their voices reach every corner of the world—because together, we can make a difference.

We hope you have been moved by the stories of courage, resilience, and hope from Palestine.

The stories in this book are a reminder that even in the darkest of times, the light of hope shines brightly in the hearts of children. These are the voices of the future—voices that refuse to be silenced, that stand firm in the face of adversity, and that carry with them the dreams of a peaceful tomorrow.

Visit www.voicesfromtheolivetrees.com to learn how you can support ongoing efforts and stay involved in future projects that aim to amplify the voices of the unheard.

## About the Authors

This book was crafted by young students from around the world, participants in the Emaan Power Rising Heroes program. Through this project, they not only gave a platform to the children of Palestine but also discovered their own strength and ability to make a difference.

We believe as these Rising Heroes rise around the world, inshaAllah together they and many others like them, will build a better and brighter, peace filled world.

Printed in Great Britain
by Amazon

46693124R00066